Everything
CAT

What Kids Really Want to Know About Cats

by
Marty Crisp

SCHOLASTIC INC.

New York   Toronto   London   Auckland   Sydney
Mexico City   New Delhi   Hong Kong   Buenos Aires

Edited by Ruth Strother
Cover and text design by Michele Lanci-Altomare

ISBN 0-439-66411-X

12 11 10 9 8 7 6 5 4 3 2 1   4 5 6 7 8 9/0

Printed in the U.S.A.   23

First Scholastic printing, November 2004

The cats in this book are referred to as *he* or *she* in alternating chapters.

All photographs provided by Getty Images,
except for page 35, copyright © 2003 Michele Lanci-Altomare,
and page 46, copyright © 2003 Wendy Lutge.

Acknowledgments

SPECIAL THANKS TO PAUL J. CAPPIELLO, DVM, Peaceable Kingdom Animal Hospital, Ephrata, PA, and Julie Adams, DVM, Conestoga Animal Hospital, Hinkletown, PA, for their help in reviewing the manuscript. Please note that any errors are the author's alone.

Additional thanks to my editor, Ruth Strother, who really knows her stuff, and to NorthWord's Aimee Jackson, who changed publishing houses but didn't leave me behind. Here's to book five together, Aimee!

Dedication

IN MEMORIAM: ROBERTO J. VIANO, SEPTEMBER 20, 1944–September 20, 2002, a man who liked cats and loved his family.

—*M. C.*

contents

Pedigreed or not, cats make
wonderful friends and companions.

introduction

A CAT BY ANY OTHER NAME IS STILL A CAT.
In Chinese, it's *mio;* in Italian, it's *gatto;* and in Dutch, it's *poes;* but it all boils down to the same aloof yet curious creature we call "cat." Breeders have tried to create new shapes and sizes of cats, but the cat has always remained pretty much the same—cat-shaped. Many cat lovers believe this is because the cat is perfect and simply can't be improved.

The idea for this book started with dogs. I visit schools and since I'm an author of middle grade fiction about dogs, kids ask me questions about dogs. I collected those questions and answered them in my book called *Everything Dog: What Kids Really Want to Know About Dogs.* But in every school I visited, there were plenty of kids who didn't have dogs—they had cats. And those kids asked questions about cats. So I started trying to find the answers to kids' curious questions about nature's most curious animal, *Felis cattus* (formerly known as *Felis domesticus*).

Cats are important to the whole history of human civilization, so let's start at the beginning.

Did cats come from dinosaurs?

When the dinosaurs became extinct, many smaller fur-bearing creatures managed to hang on and evolve, or change, into animals we know today. A small, furry weasel-like creature with good teeth called the miacid was living 55 million years ago. This was the carnivore, or meat eater, who eventually evolved into the animal with the most impressive teeth ever seen on earth—the saber-toothed tiger.

Smilodons, which is scientific speak for saber-toothed tigers, used their 8-inch-long front teeth to stab their prey. Of course, saber-toothed tigers had to eat what they caught, and those huge front teeth look like they'd get in the way. A human's jaws can open to a 45 degree angle, maximum. But saber-toothed tigers had hinged jaws that opened up to a 90 degree angle, which allowed any kind of prey past their enormous front teeth.

Smilodons were the dominant cat on earth for millions of years. But this branch of the cat family turned out to be a dead end. It was another, less toothy, branch, called *Felis lunensis,* that led to modern cats. About 12 million years ago, these smaller, more adaptable catlike creatures were the start of the Felidae, or cat, family. They evolved into two distinct varieties: *Panthera,* the big cats, who can roar because they have a small, movable bone at the base of their tongue, and *Felis,* the smaller cats, who cannot roar. (A third member of the cat family, *Acinonyx,* or cheetah, evolved from a different branch.) We're here to talk about *Felis cattus,* the most people-friendly member of the Felidae family.

About 4,500 years ago, cats got together with the ancient Egyptians. This early civilization stored grain, which attracted rats and mice. In turn, the rats and mice attracted cats. Those cats became the ancestors of all domestic cats today.

How many breeds of cat exist today?

As with dogs, different organizations in different countries (and sometimes in the same country) recognize different cat breeds. All over the world, somewhere between 80 and 100 pedigree breeds are now recognized. It's hard to pin down the exact number, since there always seems to be experimental breeds that have yet to achieve any group's official recognition. A few current unrecognized breeds are the Chinese harlequin, the palomino, the Mandarin, and the poodle cat.

The first cat show was held at the Crystal Palace, in London, England, in 1871. At that time, 25 different breeds participated. About 60 new breeds have developed since then in a little over 100 years. Cat breeds today include the glamorous Persian, the elegant Angora, the plush Russian blue, the round-eyed Burmese, and the slant-eyed Siamese. Cats can be big like the Maine coon, little like the Singapura, short-legged like the munchkin, long-legged like the Korat, tailless like the Manx, bushy-tailed like the Norwegian forest cat, hairless like the sphynx, thick-haired like the chinchilla Persian, curly-haired like the LaPerm, tufted-toed like the Somali, curly-eared like the American curl, or drop-eared like the Scottish fold. Some of the newer breeds, such as the Bengal, even have actual wild cat ancestry, bred from the wild Asian leopard cat to look like a spotted cheetah.

With cats, however, far more than with dogs, mixed breed cats (called random breds by cat breeders) far outnumber their purebred brothers and sisters. Of the whole domestic cat population, 2 percent are purebred. All the rest are mixed.

The Persian (opposite left) and the Siamese (opposite right) are 2 of the 100 or so breeds of cat.

Did curiosity really kill the cat?

Cats like to explore. And they learn quickly. They're instinctively cautious when they approach new things, but they're also ready to figure out whatever needs figuring: opening a latch, nabbing a bologna sandwich off the kitchen counter, or avoiding a toddler who pulls tails. A curious cat once survived 37 days inside a vending machine when she slipped through the food slot. A small kitten examining the end of a vacuum cleaner was accidentally sucked into the hose and survived. Curiosity does not always kill the cat, but it does give him some close calls.

Cats are known for their curiosity.

My cat doesn't come when I call her. Does she know her name?

Your cat definitely hears you. A cat's ears have pinnae, or ear cones, that turn in all directions like radar. We can't move our ears at all (okay, most of us can't). But a cat's pinna has more than 20 muscles working to allow it to turn and pick up sound coming from all sides, including from behind. A cat usually sits still to listen because it's harder to pinpoint sounds when on the move.

Humans can hear sound up to 20,000 mega-hertz (a measurement of sound). Dogs can hear 35,000 to 40,000 megahertz. Cats pick up an astonishing 100,000 megahertz. They can even hear the ultrasonic sounds that are known to precede natural occurrences such as earthquakes, volcanic eruptions, and electrical storms.

Chances are good that your cat knows her name, too. And when she believes she has some-thing to gain, she'll come when called. Although she hears you call, she's asking the question that has helped cats survive for thousands of years: What's in it for me?

A cat's ears are made to pick up sounds from all around.

Can you teach a cat tricks?

The lion and tiger tamers in the circus think you can. And think about the useful things house cats learn to do and continue to do without coaching. They use a litter pan, meow to be let out, and frequently learn to open doors. They also seek out high vantage points, sometimes balancing on impossibly small objects just to get to where they want to be. Pretty talented, these cats!

Cats can learn tricks— especially if there is something in it for them!

How much sleep does a cat need?

It seems like cats are always sleeping. And it's true that left on their own cats sleep away as much as 75 percent of any given day. That's 18 hours a day. Cats with active companions tend to stay awake more, enjoying the interaction. But remember, cats are predators in the wild, always on the lookout for their next meal. Much of the time, scientists have learned, cats sleep lightly, waking as often as every several minutes. Even in sleep, they are alert to what's around them. This is where the term *catnap* comes from. Only about 30 percent of a cat's sleeping time is spent in the kind of deep sleep human beings try to achieve when we go to bed at night.

Catnapping is a favorite "activity" among cats.

Why do cats purr?

Purring can definitely signal contentment. But that's not the only reason cats purr. They may purr to invite play, to soothe a threatening enemy, or to reassure other cats that they mean no harm.

Experts disagree quite a bit over how a cat purrs. Some think a purr is the sound of turbulence in the main vein of a cat's heart. Others think that when a cat arches his back, the blood vibrates through his body, resonating in his sinuses and producing the sound we call a purr. Most scientists, however, think the purr is the sound of a vibrating membrane called the false vocal cord, located close to the cat's actual vocal chords.

Do cats communicate?

Some people believe cats can talk, although we haven't translated cat-speak to date. They meow to signal a need for attention or food. They gurgle (a high-pitched, friendly greeting), chat (a soft meow), screech (when they're upset), caterwaul (usually a tomcat's territorial challenge to other cats), hiss (a warning), growl (a threat), snarl (a bigger threat), or click their teeth as if chattering with cold (they want their prey, or food, so badly that their mouths are already working on chewing it).

Cats also say a lot with body language. They arch their backs and raise their fur as a threat or warning and an effort to look larger. They also crouch in readiness for whatever's coming. They move their ears: forward (friendly interest), slightly back (defensiveness), and flattened (fear). Their tails are telling, too: rapid side-to-side tail movements, a bit like wagging (excitement); tail up, held still (friendly greeting); and tail up, slightly twitching (alertness, possibly

A cat can use body language and her voice to get her point across.

readying for an attack). The saying *pussyfooting around* comes from a cat's body language when preparing for a fight: approaching, backing off, coming back, and backing off again. Cats may seem silent and mysterious, but they have a lot to say to people who know how to look and listen.

Why do cats play with their food?

Cats in the wild hunt animals for food. They are good at catching rodents such as rats and mice by the tail. A creature held down only by its tail can still bite. Cats don't want to be injured by whatever they've got trapped under a paw, so a

cat "plays" with, or teases, the creature he's captured. He wants to tire it out to the point where he can easily lunge in for the kill without worrying about teeth, beaks, or claws fighting back. This instinctual behavior looks funny, however, when done with a piece of kibble.

Why does my cat stare at me?

Most of the time, she's not staring at you, she's staring through you. The fact is she's not really using her eyes at all. She's using a sixth sense. A cat uses her mouth to pull scent into a small tube just behind her upper front teeth. The tube attaches to the Jacobson's organ.

When a cat appears to be staring with her mouth just slightly open, she is using her Jacobson's organ to sample the air. This is called the flehmen response. The German word *flehmen* translates roughly into "grimacing," but the act looks more like a vacant staring into the distance, or, perhaps, at you. But she isn't. She is preoccupied with surrounding smells to which you don't have a clue. She is reading the *Odor News* in her territory.

Why did my cat bring me a bird he just killed?

He loves you. He really loves you. A cat considers dead or, sometimes, half-dead prey a "gift." A thank-you note would be nice, but it is not expected.

How old can a cat live to be?

A 1-year-old cat is considered to be equivalent to a 19- or 20-year-old person. After 1 year, the rough formula is 4 years of a human life equals 1 year of cat life. By that tally, cats are middle-aged when they're 8 to 10 and hit retirement age around 12 or 13. The majority of cats live to be from 9 to 15 years old, but a few cats have been documented living into their 30s. An American tabby cat named Puss, who lived from 1903 to 1939, died at the ripe old age of 36 and holds the record.

Some cats have lived into their 30s, but the average cat lives to be about 15 years old.

An old cat may feel threatened by his illnesses.

Why did our old cat disappear forever?

A cat facing illness or death is aware only that he is being threatened. He cannot find the source of the threat, but the instinctual response is to hide. Unfortunately, you can't hide from death. Some old cats run off not because they want to die alone, but because they think they can outwit the ultimate predator (death) by sneaking away. Sometimes they do such a good job of hiding that their human family is left wondering what happened to them.

Some cats become
addicted to catnip.

Why does my cat like catnip?

There are actually 250 varieties of catnip, or *Nepeta cataria,* all in the mint family. Catnip is an herb that contains a chemical called nepeta-lactone. It affects some cats the way chocolate affects some people. It causes a delicious ecstasy that makes them want more—and more. Just a nip of catnip can send those cats rolling, rubbing, and batting their paws at imaginary butterflies.

Some cats don't like catnip. Others can get addicted to it, ignoring their food in favor of catnip. Although catnip's not toxic to cats, "catnipism," like alcoholism, can be a hard habit to break.

Why do my cat's eyes seem to glow in photographs?

Cats' eyes are specially adapted, or made, for seeing at night, the time when most wild cats hunt. Every cat's eye contains a tapetum lucidum, a special membrane that reflects light not absorbed by the retina. (The retina is the innermost layer of the eye and is connected to the brain.) This reflecting quality gives the cat's retina a second chance to receive light, improving night vision greatly. The tapetum lucidum also reflects light back to the camera, making cats' eyes look as if they are glowing in photographs.

Why do cats seem to have a hard time getting along?

Cats aren't pack animals. They're solitary hunters, and they are territorial. But they're also sociable. If they have to share the same territory, cats organize themselves into a group, with a top cat and a next-to-the-top cat and so on. A territory can be as large as a square mile or as small as a square foot. Controlling land or a house (territory) is what puts a cat on top. But some areas in a territory, such as a couch or water bowl, are considered communal and are shared without complaint.

Cats are solitary animals, but they can learn to get along with others.

Why is my cat so picky about what he eats?

Some cats don't like to eat where there is a lot of activity. A cat dish in the middle of kitchen traffic could drive your cat away when you sound the dinner gong. And there's also the possibility that if your cat does any outside roaming, he is picking up snacks from other people, from garbage cans, or even catching something fresh. A cat may only nibble at his dinner because it's just too much food. One can of cat food equals about five mice.

A cat's sense of taste diminishes with age, making the cat seem more finicky than ever. Since a cat "tastes" smells, he prefers food that doesn't come straight from the fridge. Cold food isn't as smelly as food at room temperature. The fact is your cat isn't unreasonable. He only wants what he wants, when he wants it, where he wants it, and in the amount he wants. Who you calling picky?

Your cat may be a picky eater because he's getting between-meal snacks.

Why does my cat lick herself?

Cats spend a third of their waking hours using their tongues to groom themselves. A cat has a barbed tongue that acts like a pick to get the knots out of fur. But grooming isn't just about looking good. It also removes dead hair and skin as well as leaves, mud, and parasites such as fleas and ticks. It tones muscles, stimulates blood circulation, and provides vitamin D (which is produced on the skin by exposure to sunlight). It helps control body temperature and relieves tension. In short, it feels good, which is every cat's goal.

Cats spend much of their waking hours grooming themselves.

Why do cats eat grass?

All that grooming means some fur gets swallowed. Natural mucus in a cat's body can cause this fur to clump together into a dark mass commonly called a hair ball. Eating grass helps a cat regurgitate, or vomit up, these hair balls before they can block the cat's digestive tract.

But the most important reason cats eat grass is for the folic acid in grass "juice." In the wild, cats get this vitamin from the vegetable matter in the stomach contents of the mice and moles they gulp down whole. But domestic cats, fed on canned meat or kibble diets, sometimes need more of this essential vitamin. Folic acid helps build healthy blood and gives a cat speed and stamina.

Should we have our cat declawed?

Although veterinarians remove the claws only from the front paws, most cat experts say declawing mutilates a cat for the comfort of human beings. The surgery has been outlawed in Great Britain and in many other countries.

A cat's claws can be protracted, or extended. But a cat does not have conscious control over the process by which her claws move in and out. When a cat stretches or flexes her paw, as when reaching for prey, ligaments attached to the claws automatically tighten. This tightening pushes the claws forward and outward.

A cat's claws are exposed when she stretches out her paw.

In a normal relaxed position, a domestic cat's claws are sheathed and out of sight. This keeps cats from wearing down their claws as they walk.

Kittens learn from our reactions that we don't like to be touched with claws. While it's true that a cat without claws cannot scratch you (or the furniture), claws are a cat's main defensive weapons and an essential part of a cat's anatomy. Even cats who are only partially declawed have a hard time climbing trees and cannot defend themselves in the outside world. From a cat or a cat lover's point of view, declawing is a bad idea.

How come my cat is afraid to climb down trees?

Your cat realizes that his claws are like Captain Hook's hooked hand in *Peter Pan*. They curve and point backwards, like hooks, making them great for clinging to things on the way up. But they're not so hot for hanging on when coming back down. Cats can climb quite high, then realize that they can't get back down by jumping. And they can't climb down backwards. A cat high up in a tree sometimes feels trapped. That's why you have to call your dad or the fire department or anybody with a ladder and a bit of patience to coax the frightened cat back to safety.

A treed cat might feel trapped because he can't climb down backwards.

Do cats always land on their feet?

Cats have a remarkable ability to land on their feet by using their tail as a counterbalance. As a cat falls, she swivels in midair so her paws are pointing toward the ground. The cat then stretches out all four paws and arches her back to absorb the force of the impact.

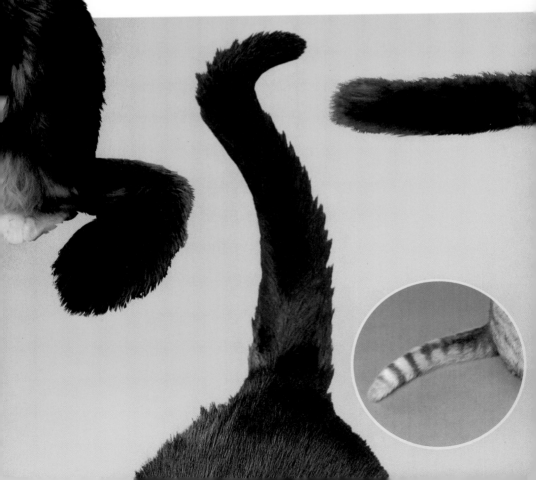

Cats use their tails while they fall to help them land on their feet.

There are countless stories of cats who've fallen amazing distances and have lived to tell about it. For instance, Gros Minou plunged an astounding 200 feet from the 20th floor of his master's Quebec penthouse, sustaining a fractured pelvis. He stayed far away from balconies after he recovered. There are also reports of cats being thrown from low-flying planes and surviving—but not without injury.

Even though a cat can right herself in the blink of an eye, a fall from a 2nd-story balcony could be tougher than a fall from a 4th-story balcony. A cat needs time to get her cushioned landing in place, and a 2nd-story fall may not allow for enough time.

Why do cats hate water?

You often see cats licking and licking themselves, trying to get every hair in just the right place. When a cat gets completely wet, the water soaks through both the outside coat and the undercoat. Try to imagine your cat licking himself dry and clean after a drenching. It can't be done. Or, at the very least, it will take hours— hours that could be better spent catnapping. A cat's coat also loses all insulating capacity when wet, and cats like to keep themselves at a stable temperature (normal feline body temperature is around 102.2 degrees). Not too hot. Not too cold.

Then there's the Turkish Van cat, the exception that proves the rule. An Angora cat from the desert region of Turkey's Lake Van, this cat loves swimming, especially if it's been raised near water. The Van has a unique coat with a cashmere-like texture that makes it water resistant. It also lacks an undercoat. When a Van goes in for a dip, he comes out relatively dry. In a desert region that regularly registers temperatures over 100 degrees Fahrenheit, swimming seems like the smartest thing a cat could do to stay cool.

It takes hours for a wet cat to dry off.

Do cats really have nine lives?

Maybe. Certainly, some cats have amazing survival stories. A Wisconsin cat named Joey was accidentally buried alive under 8 inches of concrete (proving it's not safe to be too curious when workers are pouring cement patios). Eleven days after disappearing, Joey clawed his way out of his concrete tomb, escaping with tiny nubs where his claws had been.

A California cat named Panda somehow clung to the luggage rack of a speeding car until his owner figured out why people were gesturing and yelling at her. After that experience, Panda found a new spot to sunbathe, staying away from car roofs. But Panda had nothing on Buttons, a British cat who accidentally took a 300-mile journey under the hood of a car. It wasn't until his owner stopped to check the oil that she found Buttons crouching behind the battery of the hot, smelly engine. That was a short jaunt compared to the stowaway cat who survived for over six weeks in a locked shipping container bringing a brand-new Mercedes-Benz from England to Australia.

But no other cat can beat Oscar for survival. This tabby signed on as ship's cat on the German ship *Bismarck* in 1941. Ships and cats go together, right? There are a lot of rats and mice to catch onboard, and cats get respect from superstitious sailors who believe a ship's cat brings good luck. But luck wasn't with the *Bismarck* when it was sunk in battle and its crew became British prisoners of war. Oscar, on the other hand, made it to a life raft and was adopted by the crew of the British destroyer HMS *Cossack*. A short while later, when that ship was torpedoed, Oscar survived once again and found a new home on the British aircraft carrier HMS *Ark Royal*. It wasn't long before a German submarine in the Mediterranean Sea torpedoed the *Ark Royal*. Oscar was found hours later clinging to a plank. He spent the rest of his "nine lives" in a sailors' rest home in Ireland.

Scientifically speaking, cats have only one life just like the rest of us. But they seem to have a knack for survival.

5.

6.

7.

8.

9.

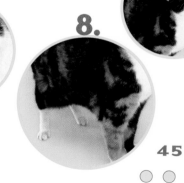

Why do cats like getting on top of the fridge?

Remember the song "Circle of Life" from the Disney movie *The Lion King?* The king addressed his subjects from atop a high bluff where he had a great view of everything around him. House cats are like our own little lion kings. They like to be at the highest point to survey their "kingdoms." Kitchens are often the heart of a house, with a lot of action to monitor. Kitchen counters make good launching pads for reaching that spot atop the fridge where a cat can keep an eye on his territory.

Cats like to watch over
their territories from
high above.

Why is a cat's tongue rough?

The upper surface of a cat's tongue is covered with backward-pointing spines, or papillae. The papillae are used for combing fur and rasping big chunks of food into smaller bits. Cats also use their tongues for drinking water. The papillae give a cat's tongue more surface area, allowing her to pick up more water than if her tongue were smooth.

The cat's nimble tongue is to the cat what our hands and fingers are to us. Many experts believe cats consider being stroked by humans the same as being licked by another cat. It goes back to the old I-want-my-mommy behavior. Mother cat washed her kittens with her tongue. The kittens liked it because it made them feel loved and cared for. Petting brings on roughly the same feelings of kittenish pleasure and security.

A cat's rough tongue is used for combing fur, among other things.

Are there any famous cats?

The most famous cats, such as Garfield, Felix, and Tom of *Tom & Jerry,* come from cartoons. Literature gives us the dashing Puss in Boots, who saves his master from poverty and helps him get the girl, and, of course, Dr. Seuss's well-loved Cat in the Hat. There is also T. S. Eliot's famous 1939 book of poetry, *Old Possum's Book of Practical Cats,* on which the long-running Broadway musical *Cats!* was based.

When it comes to real-life cats, a lot of fame seems to come from advertising. Morris, a cat rescued from an animal shelter in Chicago, went on to become a household name as the spokes-cat for Nine Lives cat food. Likewise, S. H. III, a purebred chinchilla Persian, became famous as spokes-cat for Fancy Feast, supposedly the choice of picky (rich) cats. S. H.'s fame led him to parts in movies such as *National Lampoon's Christmas Vacation* and *Scrooged.*

Disney has made a whole pride of cat movies, including *The Aristocats, The Incredible Journey, The Three Lives of Thomasina, The Cat from Outer Space, Oliver & Company,* and *That Darn Cat.* Cats often play supporting roles in movies, too, sometimes as bad guys or just pets of bad guys (think *Austin Powers* and *Stuart Little*).

And cats have found fame as news makers at the start of the twenty-first century. Rainbow is the name of the first cloned cat, born December 22, 2001, at Genetic Savings & Clone (no kidding!), in Texas. In the fall of 2001, a mother cat and her three kittens were discovered curled up in a carton of napkins in the ruins of the World Trade Center. The rescued cat family became a symbol of hope to all the workers at Ground Zero. The mama cat was promptly named Hope, and her kittens were named Freedom, Amber, and Flag.

Why are so many people allergic to cats?

Cats have dander. So do dogs. So do you, but on you it's called dandruff. Cat dander is a mixture of shed hair, cat saliva, and tiny particles of shed skin. When dander floats in the air, it triggers an allergic response in some people. It makes them sneeze and cough, and some even feel itchy. It can become hard to breathe if your body's immune system overreacts to dander.

Cat dander is more potent than most other animal dander. Cats lick their fur, adding a protein from their saliva to the dander. Licking also helps release the dander into the air. This makes allergy-prone people more likely to react to cat dander than to dog or horse or people dander. And cat dander has remarkable staying power. It's been found in houses 10 years after a cat has moved out. Statistics show that one-third of cat owners are actually allergic to their cats. Former U.S. President Bill Clinton, for instance, was so allergic to his cat, Socks, that he had to have regular allergy shots so they could both live in the White House.

Is a black cat bad luck?

No way. In the Middle Ages, however, many superstitious people started to believe that cats of all colors—but especially black cats—were mixed up with devil worship and witchcraft. Widespread persecution of cats occurred all over Europe. Cats were shot, hung, and burned at the stake. But as the cat population shrank, the rat population grew. And rats carried the bubonic plague, a highly contagious disease that wiped out about one-third of the human population. It seems as though the cat got what he likes best—the last word.

Superstitions about cats are still around today. One superstition states that a black cat who pays you a visit brings good luck, while another states that a black cat who comes to stay brings bad luck. Apparently, superstitious people can't make up their minds what to be scared of most—having a cat or not having one.

Some people associate black cats with witchcraft.

Do cats like people or don't they?

You just can't generalize when it comes to cats. Each one is too fiercely individual. Some cats like most people. Certain cats like only certain people. These members of the family Felidae, for all their aloofness and solitary ways, have adapted remarkably well to living with those strange pack animals, human beings. Do cats like people? Of course they do. If cats didn't like us, they'd leave.

Long ago cats chose to live with
people, and now they bring
companionship into our households.

strange cat facts

- The most complicated way of saying, "I love cats" is by calling yourself an ailurophile. The ancient Greek historian Herodotus first encountered cats in Egypt in the fifth century and called them *ailuroi,* meaning "tail wavers."

- The fattest cat on record was an Australian tabby who weighed just short of 47 pounds when he died at the age of 10 in 1986. He had a 33-inch waist.

- The smallest cat on record was a dwarf male blue point Himalayan, who was only 3 inches tall and 7 inches long when full grown.

- The richest cat ever was a feline named Blackie. His multimillionaire owner left over $15 million in his will to his 15 cats. Blackie survived the other 14 to become the single richest cat in the world.

- Cats were considered to be valuable mousers and ratters during the great California gold rush in the mid-nineteenth century. They were so valuable that miners paid $50 for a single mixed breed cat, which would be like paying about $1,000 for a cat today. Those miners' cats were worth their weight in gold!

• The worst musical instrument ever invented was the sixteenth century cat organ. It consisted of a dozen or so cats placed in open-front boxes with their tails poking out through holes in the back. The organ player either tugged on the tails, trying to make music with the resulting meows and hisses of protest, or used a keyboard with keys attached to spikes that prodded the poor cats. The instrument remained popular well into the seventeenth century.

• Cats have 30 teeth. That's 12 fewer than a dog and 2 fewer than a human.

• In the entire animal kingdom, only the cat, camel, and giraffe walk contralaterally. That means the right front leg moves forward at the same time as the left hind leg. Alternately, the left front leg moves forward with the right hind leg.

resources

BOOKS

ALDERTON, DAVID. *Eyewitness Handbook: Cats.* New York: DK Publishing, Inc., 1992.

BOYLAN, CLARE. *The Literary Companion to Cats.* London: Sinclair Stevenson Books, 1994.

COOPER, PAULETTE, AND PAUL NOBLE. *277 Secrets Your Cat Wants You To Know.* Berkeley: Ten Speed Press, 1997.

CUTTS, PADDY. *Cat Breeds of the World.* New York: Lorenz Books, 1999.

FOGLE, BRUCE, DVM. *The Encyclopedia of the Cat.* New York: DK Publishing, Inc., 1997.

FOX, DR. MICHAEL W. *Understanding Your Cat.* New York: Bantam Books, 1977.

Guinness Book of World Records 2001. New York: Bantam Books, 2000.

MORRIS, DESMOND. *Cat World.* New York: Penguin Books, 1997.

NASH, BRUCE, AND ALLAN ZULLO. *Amazing but True Cat Tales.* Compiled by Muriel MacFarland. Kansas City: Andrews and McMeel Publishing, 1993.

SCHNECK, MARCUS, AND JILL CARAVAN. *Cat Facts.* London: Quarto, Inc., 1990.

TABOR, ROGER. *Roger Tabor's Cat Behavior.* New York: Reader's Digest Books, 1997.

————. *Understanding Cats.* New York: Reader's Digest Books, 1997.

The Cat Fanciers' Association Cat Encyclopedia. New York: Simon & Schuster, 1993.